ENGLISH IN BLUE & WHITE

Lessons, Practice, and Resources
in
Grammar, Composition, and Literature

Chris Giles
John Powell
The Episcopal Academy

Focus Publishing
R. Pullins Company
Newburyport MA

Copyright © 2004 Chris Giles and John Powell

ISBN 1-58510-083-8

This book is published by Focus Publishing/R Pullins Company, PO Box 369, Newburyport MA 01950 All rights are reserved. No part of this publication may be reproduced, stored in a retrieval system, produced on stage or otherwise performed, transmitted by any means, electronic, mechanical, by photocopying, recording, or by any other media or means without the prior written permission of the publisher.

Printed in Canada
10 9 8 7 6 5 4

PREFACE

We wrote this book for our eighth grade English students at Episcopal Academy because we were frustrated. There was no book that did it all—no one book that covered everything we wanted our students to understand at the end of the year. Rather than using selected chapters or pages from many excellent resources, we wanted to be able to hand our students a book in the early days of September and say, "Here. This is what we will learn this year. All of it—front to back." So, we wrote one.

It includes sections on Parts of Speech, Sentences, Phrases, Clauses, Classifying Sentences, Mechanics, Composition, Literature, and glossaries of usage and poetic terms. Though it was written to be the core of the final year of middle school English, colleagues and associates have had great success using it with older students.

There has long been debate about whether studying grammar improves proficiency in or increases enjoyment of reading, writing, and speaking—our primary goals in middle school English. We believe that showing the connection between grammar and good writing helps students say what they mean.

Chris Giles & John Powell
Episcopal Academy

TABLE OF CONTENTS

GRAMMAR

PARTS OF SPEECH
- Nouns 2
- Pronouns 4
- Adjectives 6
- Verbs 8
- Adverbs 12
- Prepositions 14
- Conjunctions 16
- Interjections 16

SENTENCES
- Elements of a Sentence 18
- Parsing 20
- Complements 21
- Agreement 25

PHRASES
- Prepositional 30
- Verbal 32
- Appositive 34

CLAUSES
- Independent 36
- Subordinate 36

CLASSIFYING SENTENCES 40

USAGE GLOSSARY 43

MECHANICS
- Capitalization 50
- Numbers 54
- Abbreviations 54
- Commas 56
- Semicolons/Colons 58
- End Marks 59
- Italics 62
- Quotation Marks 63
- Punctuation with Quotation Marks 63
- Apostrophes 66
- Dashes and Parentheses 68

COMPOSITION

WRITING
- Writing a Paragraph 72
- Writing a Composition 74
- Writing Guidelines 75
- Style Reminders 76

LITERATURE

ELEMENTS OF LITERATURE 80

GLOSSARY OF POETIC TERMS 82

173 IRREGULAR VERBS 90

ACKNOWLEDGEMENTS 97

GRAMMAR

PARTS OF SPEECH

"A word's use determines its part of speech!"
- John W. Powell, III

NOUNS

Nouns name people, places, things, or ideas.

Common nouns name a general group of people, places, things, or ideas.

Kofi Annan was the **secretary-general** in 2003, the most senior **position** at the United Nations.

The Rock and Roll Hall of Fame is located in the **city** of Cleveland, Ohio.

Our new **gymnasium** is called The Dixon Gym.

A patriotic **song**, "America the Beautiful," was written by Katherine Lee and Samual Ward.

Proper nouns name specific people, places, things, or ideas.

Kofi Annan was the secretary-general in 2003, the most senior position at the **United Nations**.

The Rock and Roll Hall of Fame is located in the city of **Cleveland**, **Ohio**.

Our new gymnasium is called **The Dixon Gym**.

A patriotic song, "**America the Beautiful**," was written by **Katherine Lee** and **Samuel Ward**.

PRACTICE
Nouns

A. Label the underlined nouns with a *C* for common and a *P* for proper.

1. After leaving office, President Clinton moved to his new home in New York.
2. Brooke and Matt are coming to my house to watch the Super Bowl.
3. The sneakers seemed to have magic qualities.
4. Judge Cullen decided that both men should pay for damages.
5. Susan B. Anthony was born on a farm in Massachusetts in 1820.

B. Underline all nouns and label with a *C* for common and a *P* for proper.

1. Eric appreciated the patience and kindness shown by his teacher.
2. Sinclair Lewis, Ernest Hemingway, and John Steinbeck have all won the Nobel Prize in literature.
3. Jargon, slang, and vulgarisms have no place in formal writing.
4. Her exceptional organizational ability and keen political insight were invaluable to her colleagues.
5. William Jennings Bryan refused to allow the noise to interrupt his speech.
6. Members of the Gladwyne Civic Association met to nominate officers for the coming year.
7. *To Kill a Mockingbird*, a novel by Harper Lee, was made into a movie.
8. Chris has gained a new appreciation of opera.
9. Pedro was appointed spokesperson for the group.
10. Tamara was away over the weekend, so she recorded some of her favorite shows on her TiVo.
11. The doctor measured the man's blood pressure and took his temperature.
12. Elizabeth Cady Stanton proposed a resolution demanding the vote for women.
13. *Far Side* is a cartoon strip syndicated across the country.
14. The batter swung hard, sending the ball far into the outfield.
15. Slowly the riverboat gambler turned over his last card.

PRONOUNS

Pronouns stand in place of nouns.

Pronouns get clear meaning from their connection to nouns called *antecedents*.
Mr. Chippings likes to listen to the radio when he runs.

PERSONAL	SUBJECTIVE CASE [NOMINATIVE]	OBJECTIVE CASE	POSSESSIVE CASE
	I	me	my, mine
	we	us	our, ours
	you	you	your, yours
	he, she, it	him, her, it	his, her, its
	they	them	their
RELATIVE	that, which, who, whom, whose		
DEMONSTRATIVE	this, that, these, those		
INDEFINITE	all, another, any, anybody, anyone, anything, both, each, either, everybody, everyone, everything, few, many, more, most, much, neither, nobody, none, no one, one, other, several, some, somebody, someone, something, such		
REFLEXIVE	myself, ourselves, yourself, yourselves, himself, herself, itself, themselves		

Students may make a case for possessive pronouns being either pronouns or adjectives.

PRACTICE
Pronouns

A. Underline all pronouns.

1. Mr. Nakahara kept his collection of train schedules in a leather binder.

2. Its corners were worn from frequent use.

3. The binder contained over one thousand schedules, and each was different from the others.

4. Looking at them was looking at a study of culture.

5. Among the schedules was one with a picture of the French entrance to the Chunnel, the railroad tunnel between France and England under the English Channel.

B. Underline all pronouns and write the antecedent in the space provided. The antecedent may be in another sentence.

1. In the bullpen the relief pitchers talk among themselves as they warm up, practicing their pitches.

   _____   _____   _____

2. The pitchers practice a talent that is part art and part science.

   _____

3. It is felt and learned.

   _____   _____

4. The pitches themselves have not changed much over time.

   _____

5. However, they have probably become faster.

   _____

6. Fans who watch baseball games know the skill and labor that pitching well requires.

   _____   _____

7. The umpires, whose job requires good eyesight, may determine a pitcher's fate.

   _____

8. The decision to call a pitch a ball or a strike is theirs.

   _____

9. They are often wrong but never in doubt.

   _____

GRAMMAR

ADJECTIVES

Adjectives modify nouns or pronouns.

Modify means describe or make more definite.

Adjectives answer   Which one?
　　　　　　　　　　What kind?
　　　　　　　　　　How much?
　　　　　　　　　　How many?

"Writing is the **hardest** work in the world not involving **heavy** lifting."
—Pete Hamill

There are two articles: *a(an)* and *the*. Articles are adjectives.

A and *an* are indefinite articles. Indefinite articles refer to any one of a general group. *A* precedes nouns that begin with a consonant sound, and *an* precedes nouns with a vowel sound.

The is the definite article that refers to a particular one of a general group.

"Curiosity is one of **the** permanent and certain characteristics of **a** vigorous mind."
- Samuel Johnson

PRACTICE
Adjectives

A. In the space provided, write the word that each underlined adjective modifies.

1. _____ Some cooks use <u>many</u> recipes.

2. _____ The <u>light</u> plane made <u>several</u> attempts to land safely.

3. _____ We filled the tank with <u>five</u> gallons of gasoline.

4. _____ The 1920s have been called the <u>Jazz</u> Age.

5. _____ A <u>prizewinning</u> photographer makes certain that his <u>best</u> shots are unusual.

B. <u>Underline</u> all adjectives and articles below.

1. If one wants to see a good show of fall color, travel to New England.

2. The old jalopy needs constant attention.

3. Which player is a better free-throw shooter?

4. Egyptian pharaohs were buried in gigantic tombs with priceless treasures.

5. Some teachers are tyrants.

6. A feisty otter ruled the small pond.

7. A cold wind came up suddenly out of the north.

8. A wet summer tends to result in a more beautiful show of leaves.

9. A weathered windmill can make weird, unearthly sounds.

10. Many students read the controversial novel.

11. French cooking uses mainly eggs, unsalted butter, and heavy cream.

12. It was a glorious summer day for a picnic.

13. Eddie was nervous when he took the new job.

14. Linda did all of the hard work.

15. She was lonely and her anxious family did not know what to do.

VERBS
Verbs show action or state-of-being.

ACTION VERBS
Action verbs show physical or mental action.

It **rained** every day for a week.

She **will remember** always her first Phillies game.

LINKING VERBS
Linking verbs show the state-of-being of a subject.

The document **is** authentic.

Linking verbs link the subject to other nouns, pronouns, or adjectives.

Your handwriting **looks** legible.

Washington **became** our first president.

The most common linking verbs are forms of the verb *be*.

Forms of the Verb *Be*

be	being	will be	shall be
am	can be	would be	should be
are	could be	have been	shall have been
is	may be	has been	should have been
was	might be	had been	will have been
were	must be	could have been	would have been

Other Commonly Used Linking Verbs

appear	grow	seem	stay
become	look	smell	taste
feel	remain	sound	turn

HELPING VERBS
Helping verbs help other verbs show tense or possibility.

"We **should** all **be** concerned about the future because we **will** all **have** to spend the rest of our lives there."
- Charles Kettering

PRINCIPAL PARTS

All verbs except *be* have four forms, the first three of which are called principal parts. The fourth form is the *present participle*.

Regular

BASE (INFINITIVE)	PAST	PAST PARTICIPLE [HAS, HAVE, HAD, HAVING]	PRESENT PARTICIPLE
(to) walk	walked	walked	walking
(to) clean	cleaned	cleaned	cleaning

Irregular

BASE (INFINITIVE)	PAST	PAST PARTICIPLE [HAS, HAVE, HAD, HAVING]	PRESENT PARTICIPLE
(to) swim	swam	swum	swimming
(to) bring	brought	brought	bringing
(to) drink	drank	drunk	drinking

For a more complete listing of irregular verbs, see page 90.

TENSE

Verbs change forms to show time.

There are six tenses: present, past, future, present perfect, past perfect, and future perfect.

NAME	RELATION OF TIME OF ACTION TO NOW	EXAMPLE
PRESENT	same	I play the harmonica.
PAST	action before now	I played the harmonica.
FUTURE	action after now	I will play the harmonica.
PRESENT PERFECT	action starts before now and is finished now	I have played the harmonica for two months as of today.
PAST PERFECT	action starts before now and is finished before now	I had played the harmonica for two months before I switched to piano.
FUTURE PERFECT	action starts any time and is finished after now	I will have played the harmonica as of next Tuesday.

PRACTICE
Verbs

A. Label each underlined verb: *AV* for action verb, *LV* for linking verb, and *HV* for helping verb.

1. Susan <u>did</u> not <u>enjoy</u> the play.

2. Henry <u>has</u> <u>been</u> <u>hitting</u> home runs lately.

3. He <u>clutched</u> a script in his hands, <u>shouted</u> a greeting to some friends, and almost <u>crashed</u> into some scenery from the prop room.

4. Fred <u>has</u> <u>been</u> an A student his entire life.

5. The audience <u>grew</u> weary of the tedious play.

B. <u>Underline</u> all verbs and label them as above.

1. Go placidly amid the noise and the haste, and remember what peace there may be in silence.

2. As far as possible without surrender be on good terms with all persons.

3. Speak your truth quietly and clearly; and listen to others, even to the dull and the ignorant, they too have their story.

4. Avoid loud and aggressive persons, they are vexations to the spirit.

5. If you compare yourself with others, you may become vain or bitter; for always there will be greater and lesser persons than yourself.

6. Enjoy your achievements as well as your plans.

7. Keep interested in your own career, however humble; it is a real possession in the changing fortunes of time.

8. Exercise caution in your business affairs, for the world is full of trickery.

9. But let not this blind you to what virtue there is; many persons strive for high ideals, and everywhere life is full of heroism.

10. Be yourself.

11. Especially do not feign affection.

12. Neither be cynical about love; for in the face of all aridity and disenchantment it is as perennial as the grass.

13. Take kindly the counsel of the years, gracefully surrendering the things of youth.

14. Nurture strength of spirit to shield you in sudden misfortune.

15. But do not distress yourself with dark imaginings.

16. Many fears are born of fatigue and loneliness.

17. Beyond a wholesome discipline, be gentle with yourself.

18. You are a child of the universe, no less than the trees and the stars; you have a right to be here.

19. And whether or not it is clear to you, no doubt the universe is unfolding as it should.

20. Therefore be at peace with God, whatever you conceive Him to be.

21. And whatever your labors and aspirations in the noisy confusion of life, keep peace in your soul.

22. With all its sham, drudgery and broken dreams; it is still a beautiful world.

23. Be careful.

24. Strive to be happy.

— Max Ehrmann
Desiderata, 1927

ADVERBS

Adverbs modify verbs, adjectives, and other adverbs.

Adverbs answer   WHERE?
                          WHEN?
                           HOW?
                           HOW MUCH?
                           TO WHAT EXTENT?

Many adverbs end in *-ly*.

"I was glad to be able to answer **promptly**, and I did. I said I didn't know."
- Mark Twain

CONJUNCTIVE ADVERBS

Conjunctive adverbs connect independent clauses and are preceded by semicolons.

Commonly Used Conjunctive Adverbs

accordingly	furthermore	instead	nevertheless
besides	however	meanwhile	otherwise
consequently	indeed	moreover	therefore

Vincent studied well for his exam; **consequently**, he did his best.

PRACTICE
Adverbs

A. In the space provided, write the word that each underlined adverb modifies and identify its part of speech (verb, adjective, or adverb).

1. _____ Many students write <u>well</u>.

2. _____ <u>Yesterday</u> my sister Jo and I went shopping for new clothes.

3. _____ John <u>quickly</u> wrote his name on the application.

4. _____ The ketchup dripped <u>extremely</u> slowly out of the bottle.

5. _____ The mail carrier was <u>too</u> tired to continue his route.

B. <u>Underline</u> all adverbs below.

1. Good writers use grammar correctly.

2. No one ever proofreads too well.

3. The boxer staggered blindly to her corner.

4. The bell rang and the round promptly ended.

5. The fight promoters split the profits evenly.

6. The ring was almost surrounded by reporters.

7. Always handle a puppy gently.

8. People who have been hungry seldom waste food.

9. The first frost killed our plants too early.

10. Feed the birds in spring more generously.

11. She told her story perfectly calmly.

12. He goes to the hospital almost daily for treatments.

13. She avoided church religiously.

14. The rabbi was a deeply thoughtful person.

15. Use adverbs sparingly.

PREPOSITIONS

Prepositions relate nouns or pronouns to other words in the sentence. Prepositions begin prepositional phrases. Objects of prepositions are nouns or pronouns that end prepositional phrases.

Prepositional phrases never contain the subject of the sentence.

"No one can make you feel inferior **without your consent**."
- Anna Eleanor Roosevelt

Commonly Used Prepositions

aboard	before	concerning	near	through
about	behind	down	of	to
above	below	during	off	toward(s)
across	beneath	except	on	under
after	beside	for	onto	until
against	besides	from	outside	up
along	between	in	over	upon
among	beyond	inside	past	with
around	but (except)	into	since	within
at	by	like	than	without

Compound Prepositions

according to	because of	in place of	next to
along with	by means of	in spite of	on account of
as of	in addition to	instead of	out of

PRACTICE
Prepositions

A. Underline all prepositions.

1. Marge climbed down the ladder.

2. Felix kept tissues in every room.

3. The jet circled around the airport for two hours before landing.

4. He cut in front of her in the lunch line.

5. Instead of complaining about your grade, do something to improve it.

B. Underline all prepositional phrases below.

1. The turtle is in the box.

2. One flew over the cuckoo's nest.

3. I dropped my assignment book off the top of the Empire State Building.

4. Since that time no one calls me for homework.

5. According to Mildred, the stores were all closed.

6. The realtor walked inside the new house.

7. Many websites are written in html.

8. When the sun came up, the young soldier was still without any strength.

9. After a few days, the young man was well enough to travel.

10. In spite of giving our best effort we lost the match.

11. We must study reading and writing in addition to arithmetic.

12. Maggie found it difficult choosing between wedding dresses.

13. Before long we were bored.

14. These tickets are for Pam and me.

15. Snowball wanted to divide the windfall of apples among all the animals.

CONJUNCTIONS

Conjunctions connect words or groups of words. There are three types: coordinating, correlative, and subordinating.

COORDINATING
Coordinating conjunctions join related parts of words, phrases, and clauses.

"He never learned to read **or** write so well, **but** he could play a guitar just like ringing a bell"

-Chuck Berry

Coordinating Conjunctions

| and | or | nor | for | but | so | yet |

CORRELATIVE
Correlative conjunctions join related words, phrases, and clauses and come in pairs.

Correlative Conjunctions

both...and	neither...nor	whether...or
either...or	not only...but also	

"**Either** we have no dreams **or** we have interesting dreams."

- Friedrich Nietsche

SUBORDINATING
Subordinating conjunctions will be discussed in the "Subordinate Clauses" Section (on page 37).

INTERJECTIONS

Interjections express strong emotion and command attention. They have no grammatical relation to the rest of the sentence.

"**Well**, what are you going to do about it?"

- Brutus Bluto

"**Doh!**"

- Homer Simpson

PRACTICE
Conjunctions

A. Label all underlined conjunctions: *CD* for coordinating and *CR* for correlative.

1. The grandmother on the pogo stick went up <u>and</u> down.

2. I saw Deirdre at the ball game, <u>but</u> she did not see me.

3. You may buy your lunch at school <u>or</u> bring it from home.

4. The yearbook is given <u>not only</u> to students, <u>but also</u> to teachers.

5. My cleats are always <u>either</u> on my feet <u>or</u> in my gym locker.

B. <u>Underline</u> all conjunctions and label them as above.

1. My favorite field trip was to Betty and Bob's Barnyard Bonanza.

2. The question is whether I should review my vocabulary words or shoot some baskets.

3. Julia came in last place in the race, yet it was her best time of the year.

4. Our new class president is not only responsible and competent, but also kind and funny.

5. Auggy Doggy wags her tail, for she knows that she has earned a treat.

6. Both rain and snow annoy mail carriers.

7. Our teacher always treats us with respect, so we reciprocate.

8. That poem is neither an epic, nor is it Greek.

9. The Cape of Good Hope threatens sailors not only with treacherous land formations but also with extreme weather.

10. The squirrel that lives in that sycamore tree is usually either eating or gathering nuts.

Interjections

<u>Underline</u> all interjections.

1. Eek! There's a mouse in here.

2. Well, that's the way things go sometimes.

3. Alas! She was late for her Latin exam.

4. Zoinks! Scooby has solved another caper.

SENTENCES

ELEMENTS OF A SENTENCE

A sentence is a group of related words that contains a subject and verb and expresses a complete thought.

SENTENCE = COMPLETE SUBJECT + COMPLETE PREDICATE
(VERB, OBJECT/COMPLEMENT)

Simple subjects are who or what a sentence is about. Simple subjects are never in prepositional phrases.
Hereafter, simple subjects are referred to as subjects.

"The **aim** of real writing is to make lives larger, more alert, and, with luck, happier."
- Roger Rosenblatt

Complete subjects include simple subjects and their modifiers.
"**The aim of real writing** is to make lives larger, more alert, and, with luck, happier."
- Roger Rosenblatt

The words *here* and *there* may begin sentences but are rarely subjects. *Here* and *there* may be expletives, which have no grammatical relation to the rest of the sentence.

"**There** is nothing wrong, really, with any word – all are good, but some are better than others."
- Strunk and White

Simple predicates, or verbs*, tell about the subject or tell what the subject is doing. Verbs are the most grammatically important words within the complete predicate.
Hereafter, simple predicates are referred to as verbs.

"Writing **makes** the precise man."
- Ralph Waldo Emerson

Complete predicates include verbs, complements, and other related words.
"Writing **makes the precise man.**"
- Ralph Waldo Emerson

COMPOUNDS

Compound subjects contain two or more subjects that share the same verb.
"**A fool** and **his money** are soon parted."
- English Proverb

Compound verbs contain two or more verbs that share the same subject.
"'Tis better to have **loved** and **lost** than never to have loved at all."
- Alfred Tennyson

PRACTICE
Elements of a Sentence

A. Label the underlined elements of the sentence as complete subject and complete predicate: *CS* for complete subject and *CP* for complete predicate.

1. A large, colorful umbrella   shaded and cooled us on the beach.

2. The fabric known as batik   has a long history.

3. About an hour ago   Julie and Earl   called.

4. Have   you   written   to your Uncle Mathias?

5. Eat an apple a day to keep the doctor away.

B. Underline complete subjects once and the complete predicates twice. Circle the subjects and verbs.

1. My mother, sick and tired, went to bed early last night.

2. There is no time like the present.

3. Give me a break!

4. The precocious child may have been playing with her chemistry set.

5. One of my relatives was born in Iran.

6. The person in the passenger seat has to pay the tolls.

7. Why do we have to study grammar?

8. Jackets and ties are required in the main dining room.

9. On Thursday I brought my science book home and studied chapters six and seven.

10. Edna called but did not leave a message.

11. London and Paris attract numerous visitors every year.

12. The year 2000 came and went without incident.

13. Before leaving for the day, please cut the grass and edge the beds.

14. Most stores can wrap one's purchases and mail them anywhere in the world.

15. Where is all the information on the Internet stored?

PARSING

Parsing is breaking a sentence into components and describing them grammatically.

THE THREE STEPS

1. Omit Prepositional Phrases
2. Label verbs as AV (Action Verb) or LV (Linking Verb)
3. Label the Subject

VERB TREE

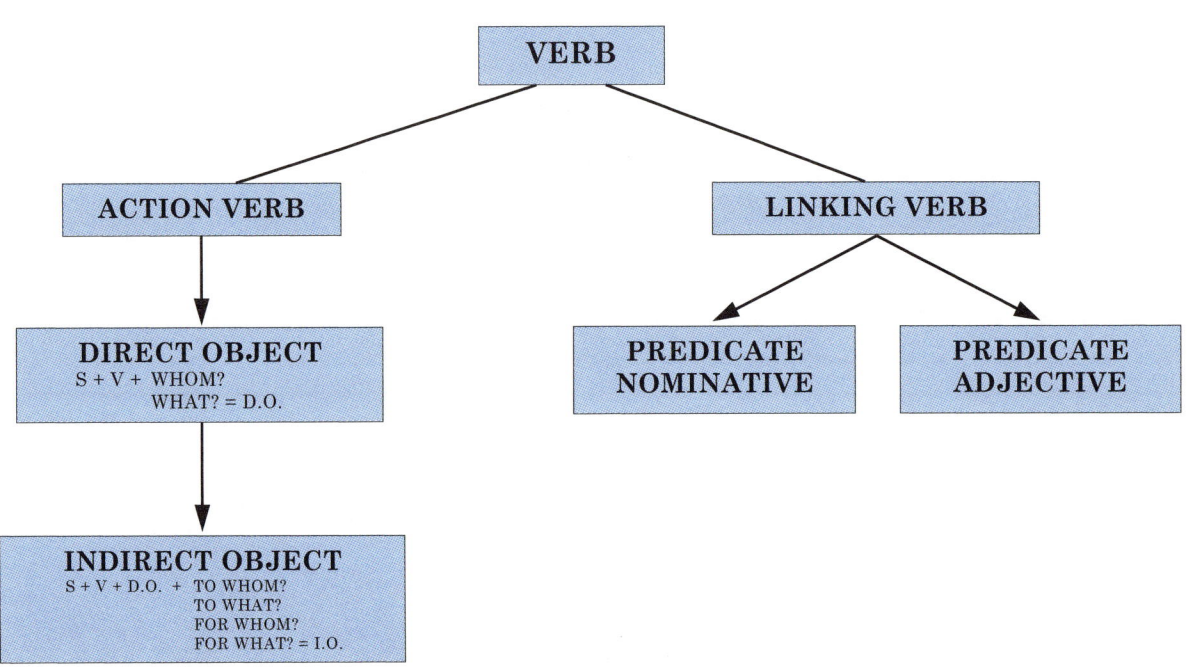

COMPLEMENTS

OBJECTS
Direct objects receive action directly from action verbs.

The teller cashed the **check** promptly.

Indirect objects precede direct objects, tell *to whom, to what, for whom,* or *for what,* and can receive the direct objects from subjects. Indirect objects never occur without direct objects.

The teacher gave the **student** the book.

OBJECT COMPLEMENTS
Object complements rename or describe direct objects.

Object complements occur with the following verbs: *consider, make,* and their synonymous verbs such as *appoint, call, choose, elect [name], cut, paint,* and *sweep.*

The team elected Susan **captain**.

He painted the barn **red**.

SUBJECT COMPLEMENTS
Predicate nominatives are nouns or pronouns that follow linking verbs and rename the subject.

Brian is our class **president**.

Predicate adjectives are adjectives that follow linking verbs and modify the subject.

The ocean air smelled **salty**.

PRACTICE
Complements

A. Label the underlined complements: *DO* for direct object, *IO* for indirect object, and *OC* for object complement.

1. We had a <u>quiz</u>.

2. The <u>Rhodesian Ridgeback</u> drove the <u>criminal</u> away.

3. The officer gave the <u>politician</u> a speeding <u>ticket</u>.

4. This spring Samantha told <u>us</u> her <u>plans</u> for the summer.

5. We thought the chapel <u>speech</u> <u>boring</u>.

B. <u>Underline</u> all complements and label them as above.

1. She wanted a job at camp.

2. The teacher gave Archie an A.

3. Most schools do not pay their teachers well.

4. Call me Ishmael.

5. The jazz combo played "Rhapsody in Blue" at commencement.

6. The baker in the corner booth sold us his fresh homemade bread.

7. In the last play of the game, the pitcher threw the ball to the first baseman.

8. She is teaching herself a new dance step.

9. The artist painted the sky gray in his most recent work.

10. He lifted his hands high above his head.

11. For a Community Service project we sent books and clothes to the shelter.

12. The riding instructor handed me the reins.

13. The middle school students read each afternoon for an hour.

14. What did they call the baby?

15. Give the Webmaster the revisions for the website today.

PRACTICE
Subject Complements

A. Label the underlined subject complements: *PN* for predicate nominative and *PA* for predicate adjective.

1. This room is a <u>mess</u>!

2. Penelope was an <u>astrophysicist</u>.

3. Melissa will become <u>president</u> of next year's freshman class.

4. The lady felt <u>faint</u> and grew <u>ill</u> at the thought of raw oysters.

5. Subject complements can be <u>words</u>, <u>phrases</u>, or <u>clauses</u>.

B. <u>Underline</u> all subject complements and label them as above.

1. This room is messy!

2. The test was easy.

3. Writing is a form of meditation.

4. George Washington was the first President of the United States.

5. The players in the photograph were Mia Hamm and Brandi Chastain.

6. Moby Dick was Captain Ahab's nemesis.

7. To many city dwellers suburban life seems dull.

8. Television is the Gobi Desert of entertainment.

9. Moose and Rocko were pedicurists.

10. What a great player you are!

11. Was Columbus the first to arrive in America?

12. The protagonist in this story seems flawed.

13. Ernie's brain surgeon looked fatigued and drawn.

14. After the picnic her pet ferret smelled foul.

15. Sheena appeared listless in rehearsal, though her performance was perfect.

AGREEMENT

SUBJECT – VERB
Subjects and verbs should agree in number.

Mia plays soccer, but **Jenna plays** tennis.

The Thompson **twins play** field hockey, but the Rodgers **twins do** not.

The number of the subject is not changed by intervening phrases.

One of the girls **is going** to the Spanish jamboree.

Reverend Zug, in addition to some vestry members, **speaks** often in church.

Some indefinite pronouns are singular; some are plural. Other indefinite pronouns may be either singular or plural, depending on their antecedents.

SINGULAR	anybody, each, either, everybody, everyone, neither, nobody, no one, one, somebody, someone, something
PLURAL	both, few, many, several
EITHER SINGULAR OR PLURAL	all, any, most, none, some

Anybody is capable of singing well.

Both of the runners **are** in good shape.

All of the tea **was pitched** into the harbor.

All of the sailors **were arrested**.

Compound subjects joined by *and* take plural verbs, unless they name a single person or thing.

Squash, cucumbers, and **green beans grow** in Tom's vegetable garden.

Peanut butter and jelly is his favorite lunchtime sandwich.

Singular subjects joined by *or* or *nor* take singular verbs.

Neither **James** nor **Bernard is** paid enough.

When parts of a subject are joined by *or* or *nor*, the verb agrees with the nearer part.

Neither my **brothers** nor my **mom wants** to go to the reunion.

Neither my **mom** nor my **brothers want** to go to the reunion.

Collective nouns may be singular or plural depending on meaning.

The **class was** quiet during the fire drill.

The **class were** writing **their** themes when the alarm sounded.

When *who, which* or *that* is the subject, the verb should agree with its antecedent.

Martha should listen to the **friends who support** her.

Martha should listen to the **friend who knows** her the best.

When the subject follows the verb, make sure they agree, particularly with respect to contractions.

Here are three **choices** for you.

There is **one** correct answer.

There're lots of choices at this school.

When *every* or *many a* precede a word or series of words, use a singular verb.

Many a ship **has** come to grief on the Cape of Good Hope.

Every student, teacher, and administrator **is** required to leave the building during fire drills.

PRACTICE
Subject-Verb Agreement

In the space provided, write the correct form of the verb. If the form of the verb is correct, write C.

1. _____ All of the ice are melting in the sun.

2. _____ Mr. Thompson, in addition to four of his students, is planning to travel to Greece for an archeological dig.

3. _____ Neither of the girls are going to New York.

4. _____ Here's the permission slips you need for the field trip.

5. _____ All of the public speaking finalists this year has excellent stage presence.

6. _____ One of the actors who specialize in Shakespearean plays are traveling to London for a theater camp.

7. _____ Milk and cookies are a common snack for younger students.

8. _____ Neither the writing contest nor the public speaking contest have been announced yet.

9. _____ Every pig, cow, and horse were inoculated against Foot and Mouth Disease.

10. _____ The referee with the mustache is the only one of the three on the field who know the rules.

11. _____ The team was loading their travel bags onto the bus.

12. _____ The team were loaded onto the bus.

13. _____ There's several ways to solve that word problem.

PRACTICE
Subject-Verb Agreement

14. _____ There have been many a day when it was hard to get out of bed.

15. _____ Either the dean or faculty members on duty calls out when recess is over.

PRONOUN – ANTECEDENT
Pronouns and their antecedents should agree in number and gender.

Singular pronouns refer to the following antecedents: *each, either, neither, one, everyone, everybody, nobody, no one, anyone, anybody, someone,* or *somebody*. The use of a clause or phrase after the antecedent does not change its number.

Each of the cities we plan has **its** good qualities.

Anyone who goes out for the boys' lacrosse team must own **his** own stick.

When antecedents could be either gender, use both the masculine and feminine forms; however, consider revision (see page 44).

Each of the **students** has finished **his or her** history paper on time.

All of the **students** have finished **their** history papers on time.

When two or more singular antecedents are joined by *or* or *nor*, use a singular pronoun.

Neither Sally nor **Molly** has **her** homework today.

When two or more antecedents are joined by *and,* use a plural pronoun.

Eddie and Linda made the Spanish website **themselves**.

A relative pronoun's number is determined by its antecedent.

Sohil is one of those **students who** are always helping **their** classmates.

PRACTICE
Pronoun - Antecedent Agreement

In the space provided, write the correct pronoun that agrees with its antecedent. If the form of the pronoun is correct, write *C*.

1. _____ Each of the girls in the cabin has to make their own bed.

2. _____ Karen is one of those girls who courageously voice their opinions in leadership positions.

3. _____ Either your father or brother has forgotten their umbrella.

4. _____ Larry Brown and the 2001 Sixers planned the celebration themselves.

5. _____ Neither Jim nor Phil has eaten their lunch yet.

6. _____ Each of the homerooms has their own rules.

7. _____ Each of the boys is supposed to bring their own pool cue.

8. _____ Both candidates brought his resumes with them.

9. _____ Anyone who wants to be a champion must prepare to practice their hardest.

10. _____ All of the best spellers have finished their preliminary rounds of the class spelling bee.

PHRASES

Phrases are groups of words used as single parts of speech. Phrases do not contain verbs and their subjects.

PREPOSITIONAL

Prepositional phrases begin with a preposition and end with a noun or pronoun (the object of the preposition).

ADJECTIVE

Adjective phrases are prepositional phrases that modify nouns or pronouns.

Thomas rescued the chipmunk **in the pool**.

Everyone **in the classroom** fell silent.

ADVERB

Adverb phrases are prepositional phrases that modify verbs, adjective, and other adverbs.

Chuck and Eliza went **for ice cream**.

The sea was thick **with sharks**.

Migrating birds fly far **from their homes**.

PRACTICE
Prepositional Phrases

A. **Label the underlined prepositional phrases: *ADJ* for adjective and *ADV* for adverb.**

1. The houses <u>by the levee</u> were all flooded.

2. The wind whistled <u>through the concourse</u> <u>of the stadium</u>.

3. The Speaker <u>of the House</u> operated strictly <u>according to procedure</u>.

4. <u>In spite of giving our best effort</u> our field hockey team lost the championship.

5. She puts Rice Krispies <u>on her chocolate chip ice cream</u>.

B. <u>Underline</u> **all prepositional phrases and label them as above.**

1. Jerry was washing the window over the kitchen sink.

2. All the children swam in the pool until dark.

3. The students in room 228 could hear Mr. Rodriguez's class in room 227 sing Spanish songs.

4. On account of the heavy snowfall school was closed for the day.

5. *David and the Phoenix,* by David Ormondroyd, was her favorite children's book.

6. Molly only missed the subway by a few seconds.

7. The miler ran four laps around the track.

8. The captured soldiers were imprisoned with little food and water.

9. On top of the kitchen counter by the fishbowl, Felix licked his paws.

10. In addition to sailing Matt excelled at windsurfing.

11. The rescuers shined the searchlights into the dark cave.

12. Over the river and through the woods to Grandmother's house we go.

13. The bottom of the mixing bowl still had traces of icing.

14. The couple seemed happy with their new home.

15. The home run sailed far over the outfield wall.

VERBAL

Verbal phrases contain verbals, their complements, objects, and modifiers. Verbals are verbs that function as nouns, adjectives, or adverbs. There are three kinds: participles, gerunds, and infinitives.

PARTICIPLES

Participles function as adjectives.

Present participles of regular verbs end in *-ing*.

Smiling for the cameras, the candidate kissed the baby.

Past participles of regular verbs end in *-d* or *-ed*.

Exhausted from the race, the marathoner collapsed.

For irregular verbs see chart on page 94.

GERUNDS

Gerunds function as nouns and end in *-ing*.

Snowboarding is Henry's favorite sport.

He enjoys **snowboarding in Vail**.

Shirley gave **snowboarding** a try.

His favorite sport is **snowboarding**.

Melissa is fed up with **snowboarding in the Poconos**.

INFINITIVES

Infinitives function as nouns, adjectives, or adverbs and usually begin with *to*.

We went **to see the exhibition**.

Arnold is the one **to see about camping gear**.

A cheesesteak is easy **to eat** quickly.

When an infinitive or infinitive phrase acts as a noun after verbs such as *see, hear, feel, watch, help, know, dare, need, make,* and *let,* the word *to* is omitted.

Jack saw the Los Angeles Lakers **win the NBA Championship**.

Unlike other verbals, infinitives may have subjects. In those cases, the construction is sometimes called an infinitive clause.

Kristen asked him **to come to the party**.

PRACTICE
Participles, Gerunds, Infinitives

A. Label underlined phrases: *PART* for participle, *GER* for gerund, and *INF* for infinitive.

1. <u>Writing from personal experience</u>, authors create their best stories.

2. <u>Exhausted by their climb</u>, the hikers stopped to rest.

3. <u>Writing from personal experience</u> is best.

4. We ran three laps before <u>leaving the field house</u>.

5. He had hoped <u>to learn writing skills</u>.

B. <u>Underline</u> and label all verbal phrases as above.

1. Approaching the curve, the car slowed down.

2. To err is human.

3. Acquitted by the jury, the defendant went free.

4. The refugees, weakened by hunger, bravely hiked on.

5. Over the summer Arnold gave sailing a try.

6. Thinking is essential to success.

7. She enjoys playing soccer year-round.

8. Known for its cheesesteaks, Pat's draws a large crowd daily.

9. Avoid the rush by mailing your holiday cards early.

10. The cargo plane was ready to fly.

11. The senator's candidacy for president is one to watch.

12. I saw Miles Davis play the year before he died.

13. A good form of exercise is walking.

14. She could see him sitting two rows away.

15. To hit Randy Johnson's fastball is a challenge.

APPOSITIVE

Appositives are nouns or pronouns that rename, identify, or further explain nearby nouns or pronouns. Appositive phrases contain appositives and their modifiers.

When appositives or their phrases are not essential to the meaning of the sentence, use commas to set them off. If they are essential, do not use commas.

Mikah will use pine, **his favorite wood**, to make the cabinet.

Her daughter **Heather** is Brett's best friend.

PRACTICE
Appositives

Underline the appositive phrase and circle the appositive.

1. My brother (Mike) is a writer living in Brooklyn.

2. My sister, (Lauren), is an investment banker living in Manhattan.

3. *Gladiator*, (winner) of the Best Picture Oscar in 2000, earned enormous profits.

4. She received her college graduation present, a (brand) new car.

5. Kajal, a good all-around (athlete), won the school award that honors the best female athlete.

6. In history class we were studying the reign of the Roman (Emperor) Julius Caesar.

7. Hector prefers to write in Spanish, his native (tongue).

8. This brand of margarine, a new (product), contains no cholesterol.

9. We (boys) must leave at once.

10. The dolphin (Flipper) starred in its own eponymous television series.

CLAUSES

Clauses are groups of words that contain a verb and its subject.

INDEPENDENT

Independent clauses express complete thoughts and can stand alone as sentences.

The players were missing easy shots.

SUBORDINATE

Subordinate clauses do not express complete thoughts and cannot stand alone as sentences. There are three kinds: noun, adjective, and adverb.

NOUN

Noun clauses function as subjects, objects, and complements, and can begin with the following connectives: *that, what, whatever, who, whom, whoever, whomever, when, where, whether, why,* or *how.*

Whatever you want to do is okay with him.

Some noun clauses that omit the introductory connective or other elements are called elliptical clauses.

I heard [that] the class might travel to New York this spring.

ADJECTIVE

Adjective clauses modify nouns or pronouns and usually begin with relative pronouns; adverbs sometimes introduce adjective clauses.

A person **who has mastered a second language** is bilingual.

Spring is the season **when daffodils bloom**.

ADVERB

Adverb clauses modify verbs, adjectives, or other adverbs and begin with subordinating conjunctions.

Whenever the jazz combo played, the students went wild.

The yoga class was difficult **because the exercises stressed her back**.

Geoff arrived a half hour later **than they did**.

Subordinating conjunctions introduce adverbial clauses and connect them to an independent clause.

"The brain is like a muscle. **When** it is in use, we feel very good. Understanding is joyous."

- Carl Sagan

Common Subordinating Conjunctions

after	even though	till
although	how	unless
as	if	until
as if	in order that	when
as much as	provided	whenever
as though	since	where
as well as	so that	wherever
because	than	whether
before	that	while
even if	though	why

PRACTICE
Clauses

A. Label the underlined clauses: *IND* for independent and *SUB* for subordinate.

1. <u>The buck stops here</u>.

2. <u>When you see Shirley</u>, please give her the message.

3. She left <u>before he could give her the message</u>.

4. <u>Michael Jordan was a great basketball player</u>.

5. <u>After she earned her diploma</u>, she went abroad to study at St. Andrews University <u>that was renowned for its Classics department</u>.

B. Underline and label all subordinate clauses: *N* for noun, *ADJ* for adjective, and *ADV* for adverb.

1. The model shows what the teacher wants.

2. Why I collect shrunken heads puzzles my friends.

3. The theme of her speech was what we thought it would be.

4. Most athletes know why smoking is harmful.

5. Because the book report is due on Monday, we must work all weekend.

6. *The New York Times* prints what is fit to print.

7. I have an aunt who is a professor at Purdue.

8. English is the course she teaches.

9. Because it was about to storm, we called off the game.

10. If we hurry, we can catch the earlier train.

11. Henry is taller than I am.

PRACTICE
Clauses

12. The team that controls the ball has a better chance of winning.

13. Here is my aunt's classroom where she teaches English.

14. Is this the painting you mentioned?

15. She played as she practiced, with intensity.

CLASSIFYING SENTENCES

BY STRUCTURE

Simple sentences contain one independent clause and no subordinate clauses.

He took his books home at the end of the day.

Compound sentences contain two or more independent clauses and no subordinate clauses.

He took his books home at the end of the day, but he never cleaned out his locker.

Complex sentences contain one independent clause and one or more subordinate clauses.

He cleaned out his locker when school was finished for the year.

Compound-complex sentences contain two or more independent clauses and one or more subordinate clauses.

He took his books home at the end of the day, but he never cleaned out his locker when school was finished for the year.

BY PURPOSE

Declarative sentences make statements.

All the fish died.

Imperative sentences make commands or requests.

Shake hands with a firm grip.

Interrogative sentences ask questions.

How many rules do we have to learn?

Exclamatory sentences show strong emotion.

The U2 concert was fantastic!

PRACTICE
Classifying Sentences

A. <u>Underline</u> independent clauses twice and subordinate clauses once. In the space provided classify the sentence by its structure: *S* for simple, *CD* for compound, *CX* for complex, and *CD-CX* for compound complex.

1. _____ Reading poetry can be exhausting.

2. _____ While reading Wordsworth, Sohil's forehead began to ache.

3. _____ It is hard to imagine what happens in a poet's mind.

4. _____ In Shakespeare's *A Midsummer Night's Dream* Theseus, the Duke of Athens, says, "The lunatic, the lover, and the poet are of imagination all compact."

5. _____ While prose has meaning, poetry explores meaning.

6. _____ Reading poetry is a jog around the park, but writing poetry is a marathon.

7. _____ Though many poems rhyme there are many poems that do not.

8. _____ A poem's theme is what it means; however, one needs to recognize the subject of a poem before one can understand its meaning.

9. _____ She claimed the theme of the poem was plain to see.

10. _____ Read a poem every day.

PRACTICE
Classifying Sentences

B. In the space provided classify the sentence by its purpose: *DEC* for declarative, *IMP* for imperative, *INT* for interrogative, and *EXC* for exclamatory.

1. _____ Duck!

2. _____ Why don't they have straws at the zoo?

3. _____ Exit the building immediately!

4. _____ Please, do not feed the animals.

5. _____ Can you speak a foreign language?

6. _____ Sweatshirts can only be worn during sports time.

7. _____ Tell the truth.

8. _____ Make-up, nail polish, jewelry, and other decorations should be kept to a minimum.

USAGE GLOSSARY

accept, except
    Accept means "receive." *Except* is usually a preposition that means "but for" or "other than." Sometimes it is a verb that means "leave out."

affect, effect
    Affect as a verb usually means "to influence"; *effect* is a noun meaning "result." Occasionally *effect* is a verb that means "to bring about."

all ready, already
    All ready means "completely prepared," and *already* means "by now" or "before now."

all together, altogether
    All together means "in unison" or "gathered in one place."
    Altogether means "entirely."

allusion, illusion
    Allusion means "an indirect reference" and *illusion* means "a deceptive appearance."

a lot
    A lot is two words.

among, between
    Use *between* with two things. Use *among* with more than two things.

and etc.
    Etc. (et cetera) means "and the rest." *And etc.* is redundant.

being as, being that
    Use *because*.

beside, besides
    Beside is a preposition that means "next to." *Besides* as a preposition means "except" or "in addition to," and as an adverb it means "in addition."

better, had better
    Use *had better* as a verb.

convince, persuade
    Convince means "to change someone's opinion" and should be followed by *of* or *that*. *Persuade* means "to move someone to action" and should be followed by *to*.

could care less
    Use *could not care less* or avoid this weak expression.

discover, invent
>*Discover* means "to find, see, or learn about something that already exists." *Invent* means "to create something that has never existed before."

farther, further
>*Farther* refers to additional geographic distance. *Further* refers to additional time or depth.

feel
>Avoid using *feel* when you mean "think" or "believe."

fewer, less
>*Fewer* refers to individual, countable items. *Less* refers to quantities or amounts.

former, latter
>*Former* refers to the first-named of two things. *Latter* refers to the second-named.

get
>Avoid over-using *get*.

good, well
>*Good* is an adjective; *well* is the adverbial form of *good*. As an adjective *well* refers to one's health.

had ought
>Omit *had*.

have, of
>Use *have*, not *of*, after helping verbs.

ROUGH	We should of won that game.
REVISED	We should have won that game.

he, she; he/she
>Masculine pronouns should not replace nouns that are made up of both genders. The construction *he/she* is ill-contrived. Use *she or he*, *he or she*, make the pronoun plural, or rewrite.

ROUGH	When a student learns rules of grammar, he communicates more effectively.
REVISED	When a student learns rules of grammar, she or he communicates more effectively.
REVISED	When a student learns rules of grammar, he or she communicates more effectively.
REVISED	When students learn rules of grammar, they communicate more effectively.
REVISED	Students who know rules of grammar communicate more effectively.

hopefully
> *Hopefully* is an adverb that means "with hope."
>
> Sandy looked hopefully into the refrigerator.
>
> Avoid using hopefully to mean "I hope."
>
> ROUGH   Hopefully the Snickers bar is still there.
>
> REVISED   I hope the Snickers bar is still there.

imply, infer
> Writers and speakers *imply* or suggest meaning.
>
> Ms. Buggy implied that the team's coach was a good motivator.
>
> Readers and listeners *infer* or conclude meaning.
>
> The audience inferred from Ms. Buggy's speech that the coach was a good motivator.

its, it's
> *Its* is a possessive pronoun. *It's* is a contraction of "it is."

like, as
> *Like*, when used as a preposition, should not introduce a clause. Use *as* or *as if* instead.
>
> ROUGH   The dance was a big success like we had hoped.
>
> REVISED   The dance was a big success as we had hoped.

prejudice, prejudiced
> *Prejudice* is a noun. *Prejudiced* is an adjective.
>
> Prejudice is born from fear of the unknown.
>
> Prejudiced thoughts are born from fear of the unknown.

pretty
> *Pretty* is overused as an adverb qualifier.
>
> ROUGH   Janelle seemed pretty terrified before presenting her public speech.
>
> REVISED   Janelle seemed terrified before presenting her public speech.

principal, principle
> *Principal* can mean "foremost" or "major" as an adjective or "chief official" or "capital sum" as a noun. *Principle* is a noun meaning "rule" or "axiom."

quote, quotation
> *Quote* is usually a verb, but can be a noun meaning "an estimate." *Quotation* is a noun comprised of the exact words that someone said or wrote.

raise, rise
> *Raise* is a transitive verb meaning "lift." *Rise* is an intransitive verb meaning "get up."

set, sit
> *Set* is a transitive verb meaning "place" or "put." *Sit* is an intransitive verb meaning "be seated."

since
> Do not use *since* to mean "because" if there is any chance that your meaning will not be clear.
>
> ROUGH   *Since* our homeroom had 100% participation in the can drive, we have not had any homework
>
> REVISED   *Because* our homeroom had 100% participation in the can drive, we have not had any homework.
>
> *Since* usually means "from the time that."
> *Since* the day Shelly was born, she has smiled incessantly.

than, then
> *Than* is a conjunction used in comparisons. *Then* is an adverb indicating time.
>
> If frozen yogurt were tastier than ice cream, then I would eat more of it.

that, which
> *That* introduces restrictive clauses. *Which* usually introduces nonrestrictive clauses and is, therefore, set off by commas.
>
> The rendition of *A Midsummer Night's Dream* that The Royal Shakespeare Company produced was fantastic!
> The newest rendition of *A Midsummer Night's Dream* on film, which stars Kevin Kline, was a disappointment.

their, there, they're
> *Their* is a possessive pronoun. *There* is an adverb indicating place or an expletive. *They're* is a contraction of "They are."
>
> Their theater is nicer than ours.
>
> The lost and found is over there.
>
> There is no one to blame but myself.
>
> They're always calling as we sit down to dinner.

to, too, two
> *To* is a preposition. *Too* is an adverb meaning "also" or "excessively." *Two* is the number.

who, which, that
    Who refers only to people.

    Which refers only to things.

    That refers to people or things.

who's, whose
    Who's is a contraction of "who is." *Whose* is the possessive form of *who*.

Your, you're
    Your is the possessive form of *you*. *You're* is a contraction of "you are."

PRACTICE
Word Usage

Underline errors in usage in the sentences below, then write the correct usage in the space provided. If the sentence is correct, write *C* in the space.

1. _____ Tiger Woods drove the ball further than Vijay Singh.

2. _____ Barry Bonds has hit more home runs in one season then Mark McGuire.

3. _____ She had a difficult choice among the two prom dresses.

4. _____ The student body were given ten nominations to choose between for student council.

5. _____ San Francisco is farther from Philadelphia than Chicago.

6. _____ The Middle Council effected change in the dress code.

7. _____ Sit your books on the desk.

8. _____ At the beach this summer we saw less people than last year.

9. _____ I feel good this morning.

10. _____ Only the principles in the play were called for rehearsal that day.

11. _____ The coach said that we should of won that game.

12. _____ Make certain to footnote all quotes in your term paper.

13. _____ Chef Familetti's cream soups are creamy, like cream soups should be.

14. _____ There are eight principal parts of speech.

15. _____ I thought I did good on the science exam.

GRAMMAR

PRACTICE
Word Usage

16. _____ Did that motivational speaker effect you?

17. _____ Who's books are these?

18. _____ You need to have ten items or less to enter the express lane.

19. _____ Your the only one who knows the combination.

20. _____ Whose on first?

21. _____ Harry cited a quotation from *A Midsummer Night's Dream*.

22. _____ Bring in you're play costume for rehearsal.

23. _____ A snake sheds it's skin as it grows.

MECHANICS

CAPITALIZATION

First word of a sentence

We were far too old to settle an argument with a fist-fight, so we consulted Atticus. Our father said we were both right.

Proper nouns and adjectives

Buddhism
Lenny
Homeric epic
Shakespearean comedy

Pronoun *I* and interjection *O*

Why, then, you left me – O, the gods forbid! –
In earnest, shall I say?

Most words in titles

Exception: minor words – articles, prepositions, and coordinating conjunctions – unless they are the first or last word

To Kill a Mockingbird
A Midsummer Night's Dream
A Clockwork: Or All Wound Up

Most titles preceding proper names

In 2002 Mayor Bloomberg replaced Rudolph Giuliani as mayor of New York.

Special cases

School courses should only be capitalized when followed by a number or when they are languages.

Algebra I
mathematics
Spanish

Compass directions should only be capitalized when naming a geographical location.

My family is from the South.

Go north on City Line Avenue until you see the Schuylkill River.

Do not capitalize seasons or names of academic years or terms.

winter
spring
first trimester

PRACTICE
Capitalization

Underline errors in capitalization in the sentences below; then write the correction in the space provided. If the sentence is correct, write *C* in the space.

1. We ate indian dishes at the restaurant called spice on third street.

   _____

2. warren said that his favorite team is the mighty ducks.

   _____

3. For my bat mitzvah uncle brad gave me a book, *Charlotte's Web* by e.b. white.

   _____

4. The best part of our labor day trip was seeing the grand canyon.

   _____

5. At military academies students take traditional classes like algebra 2, history, english, and Science in addition to courses like military science 101, and leadership.

   _____

6. Though the school is church affiliated, students come from a variety of religious backgrounds such as lutheran, roman catholic, and hindu to name a few.

   _____

7. Dr. Crawford's retirement precipitated the formation of a Search Committee to find a new head of school.

   _____

8. The national civil war museum recently opened in harrisburg, pennsylvania.

   _____

PRACTICE
Capitalization

9. The painting style known as impressionism began with claude monet.

   _____

10. The closest Planet to the sun is mercury.

    _____

11. Dermatologists have given greater attention to the effects of the sun's rays in recent years.

    _____

12. Walter Lord wrote a book titled *A Night to Remember*, which tells the story of the ill-fated ship *titanic*.

    _____

13. The internet is a useful tool for educators, nothing more.

    _____

14. A whole section of the city of hartford is known as the north end.

    _____

15. Traveling south on city line avenue took the bus driver to the Media bypass.

    _____

16. When Winter comes, certain species of birds fly South.

    _____

17. The sophomore class will hold its annual clothing drive in january.

    _____

PRACTICE
Capitalization

18. Rufus is convinced that gap jeans are best.

    _____

19. Mr. Pearson bought a Dell computer.

    _____

20. Electing a good mayor is an important responsibility for every citizen — just ask Mayor Daley.

    _____

NUMBERS

Spell out numbers of one or two words. Use figures for numbers that require more than two words to spell out and for dates and time of day. If a sentence begins with a number, spell out the number or rewrite the sentence.

Mike has six hundred autographs in his collection.

Sheila has 2,987,345 in her collection.

Twenty-two students tried out for the squash team.

Use figures for percentages; fractions; decimals; dates; addresses; scores; statistics; exact amounts of money; identification numbers; time; and chapters, scenes and pages of books and plays.

Saddam Hussein was captured by the United States military on December 13, 2003.

ABBREVIATIONS

Use accepted abbreviations appropriately.

Accepted Abbreviations

PERSONAL NAMES	Dr. Martin Luther King, Jr.
TITLES USED WITH NAMES	Mr., Mrs., Ms., Jr., Dr.
STATES	Pa., Colo., Fl., Ca.
ORGANIZATIONS AND COMPANIES	Inc., Co., Assn., Corp.
ADDRESSES	St., Rd., Ave., Blvd.
TIMES	a.m. (AM), a.d. (AD), b.c. (BC)
GOVERNMENT AGENCIES	CIA, FBI, NASA
STATE ABBREVIATIONS FOLLOWED BY ZIP CODE	Gladwyne, PA 19035
UNITS OF MEASURE	cm, kg, ml, oz, ft, yd
WIDELY USED ABBREVIATIONS (ACRONYMS)	CD, DVD, NAACP, VCR

PRACTICE
Numbers & Abbreviations

Underline errors in numbers and abbreviations in the sentences below; then write the correction in the space provided. If the sentence is correct, write *C* in the space.

1. The record for eating cheesesteaks at Jim's is 6 cheesesteaks in 30 minutes.

   _____

2. The White House's address is 1600 Pennsylvania Avenue NW, Washington, DC 20500.

   _____

3. The F.B.I.'s national headquarters is in Washington, D.C.

   _____

4. Dr L Pearcy is one of the country's leading experts on ancient medicine.

   _____

5. 16 players is the limit for the soccer team's roster.

   _____

6. Only 5 km separated the leader from the finish line.

   _____

7. Lunch begins at 11:30 am each day of the week.

   _____

8. In nineteen twenty-nine the stock market crashed.

   _____

9. Soon we will be able to record DVDs at home.

   _____

10. The "I Have a Dream" speech by Martin Luther King, Jr is widely known.

    _____

GRAMMAR

COMMAS

Between items in a series
Paula plays soccer, squash, and field hockey.

Between coordinate adjectives (adjectives that can be connected with *and*)
His mood was affected by the long, gloomy winter.

Before a coordinating conjunction joining independent clauses
His eyebrows came together, and he peered up at me from under them.

After an introductory word group
As a matter of courtesy, please turn off all cell phones in the dining room.

After two or more introductory prepositional phrases
From the look on Uncle Jack's face, I thought I was in for it again.

To set off a nonessential element
Ernie's tie, which is a clip-on, dragged through his soup.

To set off transitional and parenthetical expressions and contrasted elements
Patrick's tie, on the other hand, was perfectly clean.
Mr. Familetti serves meals that are tasty, yet nutritious.

To set off nouns of direct address, the words *yes* and *no*, interrogative tags, and mild interjections
"Mr. Referee, that was an excellent call."
"Yes," the coach replied, "I agree."
"He calls a good game, right?"
"Well, he was terribly inconsistent the last time we played."

To set off direct quotations with expressions such as *he said*
"I'll tell him you said hey, little lady," he said.

Dates, addresses, and titles
July 4, 1776
3734 Elvis Presley Boulevard, Memphis, Tennessee
Ken Griffey, Jr.

PRACTICE
Commas

Insert commas where they are needed.

1. In the winter middle school girls can choose swimming basketball squash ultimate or track.

2. The old grey mare was retired from the hunting field.

3. Of course students should not attend school when they are sick.

4. In the garbage cans behind our garage the raccoons had a feast.

5. *The Thinker* one of Julia's favorite sculptures sits outside the Rodin Museum.

6. Our bus from Tredyffrin for example was late forty-seven times last year.

7. Bobo put your red nose back on.

8. Well that was terribly rude!

9. "Ice hockey is a popular sport in Canada eh?"

10. No you may not ask questions during the exam.

11. "Touch your nose" Simon said.

12. Our address here is 1234 Anyplace Lane Anywhere MI 07413.

13. The letter was dated April 13 1980.

14. John F. Kennedy Sr. was assassinated in Dallas in 1963.

15. Although the exit polls indicated otherwise George W. Bush won the Presidential election in 2001.

SEMICOLONS

Between independent clauses if they are not joined by a coordinating conjunction

It was difficult to keep the old house clean; there was always a film of dust on the rough floorboards.

Between independent clauses joined by conjunctive adverbs or transitional expressions

Eliza enjoys playing on the tennis team; however, she would also enjoy running for the track team.

Transitional Expressions

as a result	for instance	in fact	in conclusion
for example	in addition	that is	in other words

Monica won the second heat; as a result, she qualified for the finals.

Between items in a series if the items contain commas

Play rehearsal will occur on Wednesday, October 14; Friday, October 16; and Saturday, October 17.

COLONS

After an independent clause to mean "note what follows"

When you come to field hockey practice you will need the proper equipment: a stick, a mouth-guard, and cleats.

Before a long, formal statement or a long quotation

The Middle School Handbook is explicit about lateness: "It is extremely important that our students make every effort to be in their homerooms by 8:05 AM. Failure to arrive on time in the homeroom constitutes lateness, and a late pass must be obtained from the Middle School office and then be presented to the teacher of the first class."

In conventional situations
10:15 AM
Mark 2:1-5
Dear Ms. Jones: (business)

Colons should not follow verbs.
INCORRECT   A few examples of pasta are: tortellini, ravioli, and linguini.
CORRECT   A few examples of pasta are tortellini, ravioli, and linguini.

END MARKS

Periods — used to end all sentences except direct questions or exclamations
Ralph lay in a covert, wondering about his wounds.

Exclamation Points — used to end exclamatory sentences
The building collapsed before our very eyes!

Question Marks — used to end direct questions
How many prepositions have you memorized?

PRACTICE
Semicolons, Colons & End Marks

Insert semicolons, colons, and end marks where they are needed. Do not add any words or change existing words.

1. President Bush was concerned about the spy plane incident in China he called a special meeting of his cabinet

2. Our school has summer school every summer however, many of the teachers are from other schools

3. We had to memorize some important dates in American history July 4, 1776 September 17, 1787 April 9, 1865 October 29, 1929

4. The Constitution begins with a preamble that reads " We, the people of the United States, in order to form a more perfect union, establish justice, ensure domestic tranquility, provide for the common defense, promote the general welfare, and secure the blessings of liberty to ourselves and our posterity, do ordain and establish this Constitution for the United States of America"

5. A member of the vestry read I Corinthians 13 1-13 for the lesson this morning

6. Does Penelope go to bed before 9 00 at night

7. Mr. Giles won $1,000,000 in the Publishers' Clearinghouse sweepstakes

8. The inning progressed slowly as a result, the game was canceled because of darkness

9. Over the years some of her worst Halloween costumes have been a punk rocker, Barbie, and Big Bird

10. The Director of Computer Services will be responsible for establishing and administering accounts on our server these are not private accounts

11. The side effects are not minor some leave patients very ill

PRACTICE
Semicolons, Colons & End Marks

12. As a freshman one must take four core courses   English, mathematics, history, and a language

13. He knew the tickets for the concert would be scarce   therefore, he arrived at the box office early

14. Would you like a Fresca.

15. Blue jeans have become fashionable all over the world   the American originators, however, still wear more jeans than anyone else.

ITALICS *(underline in manuscript)*
Italicize titles of works.

Titles of Books
To Kill a Mockingbird
Of Mice and Men

Magazines
Mad Magazine
Wired
Seventeen

Newspapers
Academy Scholium
The Chicago Sun
The Wall Street Journal

Pamphlets
Poor Richard's Almanac
The Middle School Handbook

Long Poems
Odyssey
Iliad
Paradise Lost

Plays
Inherit the Wind
A Midsummer Night's Dream
Les Misérables

Films
Star Wars
Titanic
Jurassic Park

Television Programs
Friends
The Crocodile Hunter

Radio Programs
All Things Considered
Car Talk
The Barsky Show

Musical Compositions
Tommy
Messiah
Adagio for Strings

Choreographic Works
The Nutcracker
Swan Lake

Works of Visual Art
The Thinker
Mona Lisa

Comic Strips
Peanuts
Kathy

Italicize Software
Microsoft Word
Inspiration

Italicize URL's
www.whitehouse.gov
www.kazaa.com

Italicize email addresses
name@comcast.net

Italicize names of ships, trains, aircraft, and spacecraft.
Titanic
the *Orient Express*
the *Enola Gay*
Apollo XIII

Italicize foreign words.
mí casa es su casa
dénouement
esse quam videri

Italicize words, letters, and figures referred to as such.
The first letter of the alphabet is *a*.
The word *Worcestershire* is difficult to spell.
The numerals *4* and *7* were reversed.

GRAMMAR

QUOTATION MARKS

Use quotation marks to enclose a direct quotation. Begin a direct quotation with a capital letter.

Mr. Powell said, "Quotation is a noun; quote is a verb."

PUNCTUATION WITH QUOTATION MARKS

Place periods and commas inside.

"Procedures, procedures, procedures," is another favorite expression of Mr. Powell's.

Place colons and semi-colons outside.

Mr. Rodriguez wrote, "I regret that I cannot attend the faculty meeting"; his note, however, included several pages of comments about the new dress code.

For our yearbook this year, these students have been nominated for "Best Laugh": Ernie Simms, Arnold Horshack, and Chris Everett.

Place question marks and exclamation points inside unless they apply to the sentence as a whole.

He said, "Do you have any monkeys?"

Did he say "yes" or "no"?

When writing dialogue, begin a new paragraph each time the speaker changes.

"It's gone, ain't it?" moaned Jem.

"I expect so," said Atticus. "Now listen, both of you. Go down and stand in front of the Radley place."

When a quoted passage consists of more than one paragraph, put quotation marks at the beginning of each paragraph and at the end of the entire passage.

The news story reported, "Late last night police discovered a broken window at the General Wayne Inn.

"The case is still being investigated. Further reports will be published as they become available."

Use quotation marks to enclose titles of works that are parts of other works.

"The Most Dangerous Game" is a short story from the anthology called *Little Worlds*.

One of the Doors' most famous songs is "Light My Fire."

Use single quotation marks to enclose a quotation within a quotation.

Mr. Trumbull said, "In reply, I will quote our Head of School: 'Recycling is a community effort.'"

PRACTICE
Italics, Quotation Marks, Capital Letters

Underline all words and word groups that should be *italicized*. Insert quotation marks and capital letters where they are needed. Be clear about the placement of punctuation with quotations marks.

1. Broadcast on 88.5 FM, the Compu-dudes is a radio show for young people about computers.

2. Michael Bamberger, a former columnist with the Philadelphia Inquirer, now writes for Sports Illustrated.

3. Charles Schulz, the creator of the Peanuts comic strip, died in 2000.

4. Homer's Iliad is the first book of western civilization.

5. In Upper School students are likely to read one of Shakespeare's most famous plays Romeo and Juliet.

6. Gregory Peck played Atticus Finch in the film To Kill a Mockingbird.

7. All My Children is an example of the wasteland of daytime television.

8. Some regard Fitzgerald's The Great Gatsby as the greatest American novel.

9. Also Sprach Zarathustra, by Richard Strauss, is the title of the classical composition used as the theme in Kubrick's film entitled 2001: A Space Odyssey.

10. Ms. Killian began by saying, the following is a quotation from Lincoln's Gettysburg Address: Four score and seven years ago...

11. The sculpture titled Rocky was unceremoniously moved from the Philadelphia Art Museum steps to the Spectrum.

12. The Middle Council wrote a pamphlet called How to Do Your Best on Exams.

PRACTICE
Italics, Quotation Marks, Capital Letters

13. In his inaugural address John F. Kennedy said, ask not what your country can do for you – ask what you can do for your country.

14. She yelled, two animals have escaped!

15. Lily wrote the President a kind email at president@whitehouse.gov.

16. Amtrak's new passenger carrier, the Acela, travels from Philadelphia to New York in seventy minutes.

17. Dance companies often produce the ballet A Midsummer Night's Dream choreographed by George Balanchine.

18. Back in the U.S.S.R. is a classic song on The Beatles' White Album.

19. Microsoft's PowerPoint is a powerful tool for presenting ideas visually, but can be boring if there is too much text.

20. Many years ago a fad emerged called New Math; soon mathematics teachers went back to the basics.

21. One can find The Episcopal Academy Middle School Booklist at www.ea1785.org/htm/Units/Middle/english/index.htm.

22. Did she say one or two?

23. There are two additional homonyms for the word there.

24. E pluribus Unum means out of many, one.

APOSTROPHES
Use apostrophes to show possession.

Add –'s to singular nouns.
my dog's collar
Bob's violin
Charles's house

Add an apostrophe after a plural noun ending in –s.
lacrosse players' helmets
students' lockers

Add –'s after a plural noun that does not end in –s.
children's books
deer's antlers

Joint and compound possession

Joint
Use –'s with the last noun only
Ron and Wanda's hardware store
Sally and Ed's science fair project

Compound
Use –'s with the last element
mother-in-law's

Contractions
Use apostrophes to take the place of missing letters and numbers.
We haven't seen her.
Chris Giles '84

PRACTICE
Apostrophes

Insert apostrophes where needed.

1. My father-in-law's decision is always final.

2. New Jersey's coastline has some of the finest beaches in the country.

3. One of the strongest women's groups in the United States is NOW.

4. Chris's credit card is almost maxed out.

5. Ron and Wanda's Launderette is in Coogee Bay, Australia.

6. Lexi wouldn't have gone on the ski trip if she couldn't bring her snowboard.

7. Some called the summer of '69 the Summer of Love.

8. The Phillies' record in 2001 enabled them to win the pennant.

9. The prize-winning cow was on the nine-o'clock news.

10. The screenplay for *Stuart Little*, a popular children's book, was written by M. Night Shamalyan, an Episcopal Academy alumnus.

DASHES AND PARENTHESES

Use dashes to indicate an abrupt break in thought or tone or an unfinished statement or question.

Red Alert – I am delighted to say – won the Grade II stakes race at Santa Anita.

"He'll be painted," said Sam, timidly. "You know how he'll be –"

Dashes can be used to mean *namely, that is,* or *in other words.*

Two modern languages are taught in Middle School – Spanish and French.

(Dashes and colons are interchangeable in examples like the one above.)

July was unseasonably cool this summer – temperatures in the sixties and seventies – for the first time in many years.

Use parentheses to enclose inconsequential material.

Chris's daughter (she loves the water) would swim all day if he let her.

Commas, dashes, or parentheses may set off parenthetical elements, depending on the degree of separation sought by the writer.

HYPHENS

Use hyphens with compound numbers and fractions.

twenty-two
two-thirds

Use hyphens when two or more words function together as an adjective before a noun.

yellow-bellied coward
good-for-nothing bum

Use hyphens with the prefixes *all-*, *ex-*, and with the suffix *-elect*.

all-knowing
ex-policeman
senator-elect

Do not use hyphens to connect *–ly* adverbs to the words they modify.

newly minted quarter
recently picked flowers

PRACTICE
Dashes, Parentheses & Hyphens

Insert dashes, parentheses, and hyphens where needed.

1. Martha Stewart is a cake baking, basket weaving, party planning expert.

2. The students had two options for their free time quiet study or free reading.

3. Three quarters of the eighth grade class went to Hershey Park after commencement.

4. Warren works all day in his garden he is a fussy gardener and has a great vegetable harvest each summer.

5. Thirty five boys tried out for the spring musical.

6. Senator elect Choi threw a party for her campaign staff and supporters.

7. We invited Robert the shyest student in the class to our party and it made his day.

8. Halitherses in Homer's *Odyssey* is an all seeing soothsayer.

9. Mrs. Aardvark invited ex President Clinton to speak in assembly.

10. "What the " cried Elizabeth as the door slammed shut.

COMPOSITION

WRITING

DEVELOPMENT	DRAFT	REVISION
brainstorming organizing outlining mapping	writing	rethinking editing proofreading rewriting

WRITING A PARAGRAPH

A paragraph contains related sentences that express a main idea or thesis. A paragraph has three main parts: a topic sentence; body; and a clincher or transitional sentence.

The topic sentence presents the main idea.

> **There are two kinds of writing: good writing and bad writing.** Good writing informs, describes, persuades, or tells a story. Good writing is marked by accuracy and clarity, and you never have to guess or intuit where the writer is taking you, or how she draws certain conclusions. Remember, the key is not that you like or agree with what you read, but that you understand it! Bad writing is the opposite of good writing. With bad writing, the reader has difficulty following the writer—there are no roadmaps taking you from point A to point B, the word choice is all wrong, and there are logical craters and inconsistencies waiting to trip the reader. Be kind and attentive to your reader. If you lose your reader, then your writing has failed.

The body contains sentences that develop the main idea with supporting details.

> There are two kinds of writing: good writing and bad writing. **Good writing informs, describes, persuades, or tells a story. Good writing is marked by accuracy and clarity, and you never have to guess or intuit where the writer is taking you, or how she draws certain conclusions. Remember, the key is not that you like or agree with what you read, but that you understand it! Bad writing is the opposite of good writing. With bad writing, the reader has difficulty following the writer—there are no roadmaps taking you from point A to point B, the word choice is all wrong, and there are logical craters and inconsistencies waiting to trip the reader.** Be kind and attentive to your reader. If you lose your reader, then your writing has failed.

The clincher wraps up the paragraph.

> There are two kinds of writing: good writing and bad writing. Good writing informs, describes, persuades, or tells a story. Good writing is marked by accuracy and clarity, and you never have to guess or intuit where the writer is taking you, or how she draws certain conclusions. Remember, the key is not that you like or agree with what you read, but that you understand it! Bad writing is the opposite of good writing. With bad writing, the reader has difficulty following the writer—there are no roadmaps taking you from point A to point B, the word choice is all wrong, and there are logical craters and inconsistencies waiting to trip the reader. Be kind and attentive to your reader. **If you lose your reader, then your writing has failed.**

— *Adolphus Levi Williams, Jr.*

The transitional sentences smoothly connect paragraphs.

Mount Everest is the highest place on Earth one can go without leaving the ground. Many have been tempted to stand on the roof of the world, as the summit is often called. Enough people have tried, and want to try, that there is a viable commercial enterprise. For a very high fee experienced mountaineers can guide less experienced climbers up the mountain. Eventually that led to more inexperienced people trying to climb Everest, thinking that they would be helped and shepherded all the way up the mountain by their guides. This is false because Everest is such a challenge that even the best climbers in the world have trouble. Yet people kept on coming, and their money fueled more expeditions. Also, the lack of major accidents on the mountain led people to believe that it was easy and that all they had to do was sign up and climb. ***Into Thin* Air by John Krakauer examines the first time that the inevitable occurred, and Death visited Everest in greater numbers than ever before.**

The author, who worked for *Outside* magazine, was asked if he would like to climb Everest and write an article on the experience. As a boy, he had dreamed of climbing Everest, so he succumbed to his dream. This book follows him from the airplane to Nepal, up Mount Everest, and back down again. The climb up was without much excitement, but in the late afternoon on the day of the summit attempt, a storm broke. Many climbers were stuck on the open face of the mountain, high above safety, many without oxygen. The author tells about his struggle to stay alive, along with the other people who were climbing with him in April 1996.

— *Alex Nakahara*

WRITING A COMPOSITION

TITLE
Find a creative way to attract the reader's attention and interest.

Capitalize the first word and all the important words that follow.

INTRODUCTION
Begin with a sentence that captures the reader's attention.

Give background information on the topic.

Enhance the paragraph with an interesting example, surprising statistic, or other hook.

Include a thesis statement that conveys the main point or points of the essay.

BODY PARAGRAPH #1
Begin with a topic sentence that states the main point of the paragraph and relates it to the thesis statement.

Fill with well-chosen examples, quotations, comparisons, analogies, and / or narration.

May end with a transition.

BODY PARAGRAPH #2
Begin with a topic sentence that states the main point of the paragraph and relates it to the thesis statement.

Fill with well organized examples, quotations, comparisons, analogies, and / or narration.

May end with a transition.

BODY PARAGRAPH #3
Begin with a topic sentence that states the main point of the paragraph and relates it to the thesis statement.

Fill with well organized examples, quotations, comparisons, analogies, and / or narration.

May end with a transition.

CONCLUSION
Echo the thesis statement without simply repeating it.

May pose a question for future thought or suggest a course of action.

May include a detail or example from the introduction to tie up the essay.

End with a strong image or bit of wit.

WRITING GUIDELINES

PURPOSE
Establish your purpose early in your thesis statement and maintain that focus throughout your work. Demonstrate an awareness of your audience and task: to describe, explain, compare and contrast, define, evaluate, classify, or tell a story. Use interesting introductions and conclusions to strengthen purpose.

ORGANIZATION
Arrange your paragraphs sensibly; maintain coherence. Within each paragraph, arrange the details that support your main idea (topic sentence) effectively. Make smooth, clear transitions between sentences and paragraphs.

DETAILS
Include observations, quotations, citations, and insights that help develop your focus and interest your audience. Write with thoughtfully chosen nouns and verbs.

STYLE
Use the active voice in most of your writing; use the passive voice sparingly. Vary the structure and length of your sentences.

GRAMMAR / USAGE / MECHANICS / FORMAT
Spell, capitalize, punctuate, and choose your words with care. Always proofread. Beware homonyms (especially when using spell-check). Make subjects agree with verbs, and pronouns agree with their antecedents. Use an appropriate manuscript format.

STYLE REMINDERS

Be precise.
ROUGH   We had a successful field hockey season last year.
REVISED   Last year our field hockey record was 7 and 0.

Write with nouns and verbs.
ROUGH   The listeners laughed ecstatically at his funny joke.
REVISED   The listeners howled and swatted their thighs at his joke about the monkfish.

Avoid qualifiers.
ROUGH   Our Latin test was very difficult.
REVISED   Our Latin test was difficult.

Avoid contractions.
ROUGH   Jason can't give his public speech today.
REVISED   Jason cannot give his public speech today.

Use the active voice.
ROUGH   A decision about lunch recess was made by Principal Frankenstein.
REVISED   Principal Frankenstein made a decision about lunch recess.

Avoid fancy words.
ROUGH   Students must utilize cash to buy lunch in the cafeteria.
REVISED   Students must use cash to buy lunch in the cafeteria.

Say things in a positive way.
ROUGH   I did not remember to bring in my poster for science class.
REVISED   I forgot my science poster.

Show. Do not tell.
ROUGH   She showed satisfaction as she took possession of her well-earned reward.
REVISED   She smiled as she pocketed the coin.

Avoid slang.

ROUGH   Jenny's description of Ebola virus totally grossed me out.

REVISED   Jenny's description of Ebola virus disgusted me.

Vary sentence length and construction.

ROUGH   Anxiously looking through the day's mail, Gwen pawed through the bills and assorted junk mail until the piece with the important return address turned up. Her fingers fumbled as she tore open the letter, and while reading the opening paragraph, her heart sank.

REVISED   Anxiously looking through the day's mail, Gwen pawed through the bills and assorted junk mail until the piece with the important return address turned up. Her fingers fumbled as she tore open the thin letter. She read the opening paragraph. Her heart sank.

Put emphatic words at the end.

ROUGH   It is crucial to be thorough when reading directions for a test.

REVISED   When reading directions for a test, it is crucial to be thorough.

Avoid successive, loose constructions. Do not rely on compound constructions joined by *and*.

ROUGH   The soccer tournament took place last weekend, and a large crowd was in attendance. Our team scored the most goals, and one of our strikers won most valuable player.

REVISED   A large crowd attended the soccer tournament last weekend. Our team scored the most goals, and one of our strikers won most valuable player.

Express coordinate ideas in similar form.

ROUGH   People who do not eat lunch often exhibit one of the following symptoms: withdrawal, rebelliousness, and they are depressed.

REVISED   People who do not eat lunch often exhibit one of the following symptoms: withdrawal, rebelliousness, and depression.

Avoid clichés.

ROUGH   A healthful lifestyle enhances your ability to go for the gold.

REVISED   Living healthfully helps you perform well.

Omit needless words.

ROUGH   The biota exhibited a one hundred percent mortality response.

REVISED   All the fish died.

LITERATURE

ELEMENTS OF LITERATURE

PLOT
Plot is the term for the events, actions, or conflicts of a story.
> What happens?
>
> What conflicts occur?

SETTING
Setting is the place where the action happens.
> Does the place contribute to the story?

CHARACTERS
Characters are the people in the story, including the narrator.
> Who is in the story?
>
> How do they interact?
>
> How do their actions, words, and thoughts reveal their character?
>
> Do they change? How? Why?

POINT OF VIEW
Point of view is the perspective or attitude of the narrator.
> **First person** = a participant, using *I*, who may be reliable or unreliable
>
> **Third person** = an outsider, using *he, she, it, they*, who may be
>
> **omniscient** (knows what goes on in all characters' minds), **limited** (knows what going on in the mind of only one or two characters), or **objective** (knows only what is external to the characters)
>
> Who is the narrator?
>
> How does the narrator's point of view affect the story?

TONE
Tone is the narrator's attitude.
> What tones do you hear? Are they formal, informal, somber, playful, ironic, or condescending? Do they change? How? Why?

IMAGERY
Imagery is the use of word pictures to create sensory impressions (sight, sound, smell, taste, touch).
> What images does the writer use?
>
> Are there patterns of images?
>
> What is the significance of the imagery?

LITERATURE

SYMBOLISM
Symbolism is the term for concrete things representing larger and more abstract ideas.

    What symbols does the author use?

    What do they mean?

FORM
Form is the shape or structure of the story.

    What shape does the pattern of events take?

THEME
Theme is the central idea of the story. Theme is not plot.

    Why did the author write the story?

GLOSSARY OF POETIC TERMS

Alliteration is the repetition of initial consonant sounds.
> *perfectly polished prose*

Allusion is a reference to historic, literary, or mythological symbols or characters.
> *Pandora's Box*

Assonance is the repetition of vowel sounds.
> *nearest and dearest*

Blank verse is unrhymed poetry usually written in iambic pentameter.
> *The buzz saw snarled and rattled in the yard*
> *And made dust and dropped stove-length sticks of wood,*
> *Sweet-scented stuff when the breeze drew across it.*
>   - Frost, "Out, out - "

Cacophony is a combination of harsh sounds.
> *Bent double, like old beggars under sacks,*
> *Knock-kneed, coughing like hags, we cursed through sludge.*
>   - Owen, "Dulce et Decorum Est"

Connotation is the suggested meanings of a word — as opposed to denotation, the dictionary definition.
> *house, home*

Consonance is the repetition of final consonant sounds.
> *odds and ends*

Couplet is a two-line stanza with end rhymes.
> *The world stands out on either side*
> *No wider than the heart is wide.*
>   - Millay, "Renascence"

Denotation is the dictionary definition of a word.
> *house, home*

Diction is word choice.

Euphony is combination of pleasant sounds.

> *The way a crow*
> *Shook down on me*
> *The dust of snow*
> *From a hemlock tree*
>
> *Has given my heart*
> *A change of mood*
> *And saved some part*
> *Of a day I had rued.*
>
> -Frost, "Dust of Snow"

Figurative language is a way of using words beyond their literal meaning. There are many figures of speech; for example, simile, metaphor, and personification.

> *My heart is broken.*

Free verse is poetry that does not have a regular form or rhythm and usually has no rhyme.

> *THIS is the hour, O soul, thy free flight into wordless,*
> *Away from books, away from art, the day erased, the lesson done,*
> *Thee fully forth emerging, silent, gazing, pondering the themes*
> *thou lovest best:*
> *Night, sleep, death, and the stars*
>
> - Whitman, "A Clear Midnight"

Haiku is a Japanese poetic form with three lines. The first line has five syllables, the second has seven, and the third has five.

> *As the spring rains fall,*
> *   soaking in them, on the roof*
> *   is a child's rag ball.*
>
> - Buson

Hyperbole is exaggeration for emphasis.

> *He clasps the crag with crooked hands;*
> *Close to the sun in lonely lands,*
> *Ring'd with the azure world, he stands.*
> *The wrinkled sea beneath him crawls;*
> *He watches from his mountain walls,*
> *And like a thunderbolt he falls.*
>
> - Lord Tennyson, "The Eagle"

Imagery is the term for the creation of sensory impressions (sight, sound, smell, taste, touch).

> ALL things bright and beauteous,
> All creatures great and small,
> All things wise and wondrous,
> The LORD GOD made them all.
>
> Each little flower that opens,
> Each little bird that sings,
> He made their glowing colours,
> He made their tiny wings.
>
> The rich man in his castle,
> The poor man at his gate,
> GOD made them, high or lowly,
> And ordered their estate.
>
> The purple-headed mountain,
> The river running by,
> The sunset, and the morning,
> That brightens up the sky,
>
> The cold wind in the winter,
> The pleasant summer sun,
> The ripe fruits in the garden,
> He made them every one.
>
> The tall trees in the greenwood,
> The meadows where we play,
> The rushes by the water,
> We gather every day;—
>
> He gave us eyes to see them,
> And lips that we might tell,
> How great is GOD Almighty,
> Who has made all things well.
>   - Alexander, "All Things Bright and Beauteous"

Irony is the use of words to mean the opposite of what they say.

> Lend him to stroke these blind, blunt bullet heads
> Which long to nuzzle in the hearts of lads...
>   - Owen, "Arms and the Boy"

Metaphor is a figure of speech that indirectly compares two unlike things.

> That exam was a piece of cake.

Meter is the division of the poetic line into equal units or feet that create rhythm.

Name of foot	Name of Meter	Example
iamb	iambic	rĕ-móve
trochee	trochaic	ár-rŏw
anapest	anapestic	cŏn-tră-díct
dactyl	dactylic	múr-mŭr-ĭng

monometer	one foot
dimeter	two feet
trimeter	three feet
tetrameter	four feet
pentameter	five feet
hexameter	six feet
heptameter	seven feet
octameter	eight feet

Iambic tetrameter	Ŏ beáu | tĭ-fúl | fŏr spá | cĭous skíes
Iambic trimeter	Fŏr am | bĕr wáves |ŏf gráin
Iambic pentameter	The wórk | ŏf hún-tĕrs ĭs | ă-nó | thĕr thing
Iambic dimeter	Yŏur grief | aňd míne
	Mŭst iň | tĕr-twíne
Trochaic tetrameter	Súr-gĕons | múst bĕ | vé-rў | care-fŭl

Metonymy is the substitution of the name of an object closely associated with a word for the word itself.

The White House (substituted for the President)

Muses are the nine goddesses in Greek mythology who presided over the arts and sciences and who were thought to inspire.

Calliope is the muse of epic poetry.

Onomatopoeia is term for words that suggest their meaning by their sound.

buzz, whirr, cock-a-doodle-doo, quack

Paradox is a seemingly self-contradictory statement that may have truth.

For when I am weak, then I am strong.
                        - 2 Corinthians

Personification is representing an inanimate object with human qualities.

The cold hand of Death, Mother Nature

Quatrain is a stanza of four lines.

Whenever Richard Cory went down town,
We people on the pavement looked at him:
He was a gentleman from sole to crown,
Clean favored, and imperially slim.

- Edwin Arlington Robinson, "Richard Cory"

Refrain is a line or stanza that is repeated for effect.

'Tis a lesson you should heed,
   Try, try again;
If at first you don't succeed,
   Try, try again;
Then your courage should appear,
For, if you will persevere,
You will conquer, never fear;
   Try, try again.

- Palmer, "Try, try again"

Rhyme is the repetition of identical or similar sounds.

   IF you can keep your head when all about you
Are losing theirs and blaming it on you;
   If you can trust yourself when all men doubt you,
But make allowances for their doubting too:
   If you can wait and not be tired by waiting,
Or, being lied about, don't deal in lies,
   Or being hated don't give way to hating,
And yet don't look too good, nor talk too wise;

   If you can dream—and not make dreams your master;
If you can think—and not make thoughts your aim,
   If you can meet with Triumph and Disaster
And treat those two impostors the same;
   If you can bear to hear the truth you've spoken
Twisted by knaves to make a trap for fools,
   Or watch the things you gave your life to, broken,
And stoop and build 'em up with worn-out tools;

   If you can make one heap of all your winnings
And risk it on one turn of pitch-and-toss,
   And lose, and start again at your beginnings,
And never breath a word about your loss:
   If you can force your heart and nerve and sinew
To serve your turn long after they are gone,
   And so hold on when there is nothing in you
Except the Will which says to them: "Hold on!"

   If you can talk with crowds and keep your virtue,
Or walk with Kings—nor lose the common touch,
   If neither foes nor loving friends can hurt you,
If all men count with you, but none too much:
   If you can fill the unforgiving minute

With sixty seconds' worth of distance run,
*　　Yours is the Earth and everything that's in it,*
And—which is more—you'll be a Man, my son!
*　　　　　　　　- Kipling, "If"*

Rhythm is a pattern of accented and unaccented syllables within a recurring beat or cycle.

I sat next the Duchess at tea.
It was just as I feared it would be:
*　　Her rumblings abdominal*
*　　Were simply abominable,*
And everyone thought it was me.

Scansion is the study of the metrical pattern of verse, dividing the line into feet and meter.

Mý lóve | ĭs ás | ă fé | vĕr lóng | ĭng stíll
*　　　　　　　　- Shakespeare*

Simile is a figure of speech that directly compares two unlike things, usually with *like, as* or *than.*

Like a small gray
coffeepot
sits the squirrel.
*　　　　　　- Wolfe, "The Gray Squirrel"*

Sonnet is a poetic form with a strict structure: fourteen lines of iambic pentameter with a concluding couplet.

Let me not to the marriage of true minds
Admit impediments; love is not love
Which alters when it alteration finds,
Or bends with the remover to remove.
O, no, it is an ever-fixèd mark
That looks on tempests and is never shaken;
It is the star to every wand'ring bark,
Whose worth's unknown, although his height be taken.
Love's not Time's fool, though rosy lips and cheeks
Within his bending sickle's compass come;
Love alters not with his brief hours and weeks,
But bears it out even to the edge of doom.
*　　If this be error and upon me proved,*
*　　I never writ, nor no man ever loved.*
*　　　　　　　　- Shakespeare*

Stanza is regular grouping of two or more lines of poetry to form divisions.

In a cabin, in a canyon,
An excavation for a mine;
Dwelt a miner, a Forty-niner,
And his daughter Clementine.

Oh my darling, oh my darling,
Oh my darling Clementine,
You are lost and gone forever,
Drefful sorry, Clementine.

She drove her ducklets to the river,
Ev'ry morning just at nine;
She stubb'd her toe against a sliver,
And fell into the foaming brine.

I saw her lips above the water,
Blowing bubbles soft and fine;
Alas for me, I was no swimmer,
And so I lost my Clementine.

Symbol is something concrete that stands for something abstract.

O CAPTAIN! My Captain, our fearful trip is done,
The ship has weather'd every rack, the prize we sought is won,
The port is near, the bells I hear, the people all exulting,
While follow eyes the steady keel, the vessel grim and daring;
    But O heart! Heart! Heart!
      O the bleeding drops of red,
        Where on the deck my Captain lies,
        Fallen cold and dead.
O Captain! My Captain! Rise up and hear the bells;
Rise up—for you the flag is flung—for you the bugle trills,
For you bouquets and ribbon'd wreaths—for you the shores a-crowding,
For you they call, the swaying mass, their eager faces turning;
    Here Captain! Dear Father!
      The arm beneath your head!
        It is some dream that on the deck,
        You've fallen cold and dead.
My Captain does not answer, his lips are pale and still,
My father does not feel my arm, he has no pulse or will,
The ship is anchor'd safe and sound, its voyage closed and done,
From fearful trip the victor ship comes in with object won;
    Exult, O shores and ring, O bells!
      But I with mournful tread,
        Walk the deck my Captain lies,
        Fallen cold and dead.
          - Whitman, "O Captain! My Captain!"

Synecdoche is a figure of speech in which the part of a thing represents the whole.

> *Tell me not, Sweet, I am unkind,*
> *That from the nunnery*
> *Of thy chaste breast and quiet mind*
> *To war and arms I fly.*
> - Lovelace, "To Lucasta"

173 IRREGULAR VERBS

(INFINITIVE) BASE	PAST	PAST PARTICIPLE	PRESENT PARTICIPLE
(to) awake	awoke	awoken	awaking
(to) be	was, were	been	being
(to) bear	bore	born	bearing
(to) beat	beat	beaten	beating
(to) become	became	become	becoming
(to) begin	began	begun	beginning
(to) bend	bent	bent	bending
(to) beset	beset	beset	besetting
(to) bet	bet	bet	betting
(to) bid	bid	bid	bidding
(to) bind	bound	bound	binding
(to) bite	bit	bitten	biting
(to) bleed	bled	bled	bleeding
(to) blow	blew	blown	blowing
(to) break	broke	broken	breaking
(to) breed	bred	bred	breeding
(to) bring	brought	brought	bringing
(to) broadcast	broadcast	broadcast	broadcasting
(to) build	built	built	building
(to) burn	burned/burnt	burned/burnt	burning
(to) burst	burst	burst	bursting
(to) buy	bought	bought	buying
(to) cast	cast	cast	casting
(to) catch	caught	caught	catching
(to) choose	chose	chosen	choosing
(to) cling	clung	clung	clinging
(to) come	came	come	coming
(to) cost	cost	cost	costing

(to) creep	crept	crept	creeping
(to) cut	cut	cut	cutting
(to) deal	dealt	dealt	dealing
(to) dig	dug	dug	digging
(to) dive	dived/dove	dived	diving
(to) do	did	done	doing
(to) draw	drew	drawn	drawing
(to) dream	dreamed/dreamt	dreamed/dreamt	dreaming
(to) drive	drove	driven	driving
(to) drink	drank	drunk	drinking
(to) eat	ate	eaten	eating
(to) fall	fell	fallen	falling
(to) feed	fed	fed	feeding
(to) feel	felt	felt	feeling
(to) fight	fought	fought	fighting
(to) find	found	found	finding
(to) fit	fit	fit	fitting
(to) flee	fled	fled	fleeing
(to) fling	flung	flung	flinging
(to) fly	flew	flown	flying
(to) forbid	forbade	forbidden	forbidding
(to) forget	forgot	forgotten	forgetting
(to) forgive	forgave	forgiven	forgiving
(to) forsake	forsook	forsaken	forsaking
(to) freeze	froze	frozen	freezing
(to) get	got	gotten	getting
(to) give	gave	given	giving
(to) go	went	gone	going
(to) grind	ground	ground	grinding
(to) grow	grew	grown	growing
(to) hang	hung	hung	hanging

(to) have	had	had	having
(to) hear	heard	heard	hearing
(to) hide	hid	hidden	hiding
(to) hit	hit	hit	hitting
(to) hold	held	held	holding
(to) hurt	hurt	hurt	hurting
(to) keep	kept	kept	keeping
(to) kneel	knelt	knelt	kneeling
(to) knit	knit	knit	knitting
(to) know	knew	known	knowing
(to) lay	laid	laid	laying
(to) lead	led	led	leading
(to) leap	leaped/leapt	leaped/leapt	leaping
(to) learn	learned/learnt	learned/learnt	learning
(to) leave	left	left	leaving
(to) lend	lent	lent	lending
(to) let	let	let	letting
(to) lie	lay	lain	lying
(to) light	lit	lighted	lighting
(to) lose	lost	lost	losing
(to) make	made	made	making
(to) mean	meant	meant	meaning
(to) meet	met	met	meeting
(to) misspell	misspelled or misspelt	misspelled or misspelt	misspelling
(to) mistake	mistook	mistaken	mistaking
(to) mow	mowed	mowed/mown	mowing
(to) overcome	overcame	overcome	overcoming
(to) overthrow	overthrew	overthrown	overthrowing
(to) owe	owed	owed	owing
(to) pay	paid	paid	paying
(to) plead	pleaded or pled	pleaded or pled	pleading

(to) prove	proved	proved or proven	proving
(to) put	put	put	putting
(to) quit	quit	quit	quitting
(to) read	read	read	reading
(to) rid	rid	rid	ridding
(to) ride	rode	ridden	riding
(to) ring	rang	rung	ringing
(to) rise	rose	risen	rising
(to) run	ran	run	running
(to) saw	sawed	sawed/sawn	sawing
(to) say	said	said	saying
(to) see	saw	seen	seeing
(to) seek	sought	sought	seeking
(to) sell	sold	sold	selling
(to) send	sent	sent	sending
(to) set	set	set	setting
(to) sew	sewed	sewed/sewn	sewing
(to) shake	shook	shaken	shaking
(to) shave	shaved	shaved/shaven	shaving
(to) shear	sheared	sheared/shorn	shearing
(to) shed	shed	shed	shedding
(to) shine	shone	shone	shining
(to) shoe	shoed	shoed/shod	shoeing
(to) shoot	shot	shot	shooting
(to) show	showed	showed/shown	showing
(to) shrink	shrank	shrunk	shrinking
(to) shut	shut	shut	shutting
(to) sing	sang	sung	singing
(to) sink	sank	sunk	sinking
(to) sit	sat	sat	sitting
(to) slay	slew	slain	slaying

(to) sleep	slept	slept	sleeping
(to) slide	slid	slid	sliding
(to) sling	slung	slung	slinging
(to) slit	slit	slit	slitting
(to) smite	smote	smitten	smiting
(to) sow	sowed	sowed/sown	sowing
(to) speak	spoke	spoken	speaking
(to) speed	sped	sped	speeding
(to) spend	spent	spent	spending
(to) spill	spilled/spilt	spilled/spilt	spilling
(to) spin	spun	spun	spinning
(to) spit	spit	spit	spitting
(to) split	split	split	splitting
(to) spread	spread	spread	spreading
(to) spring	sprang	sprung	springing
(to) stand	stood	stood	standing
(to) steal	stole	stolen	stealing
(to) stick	stuck	stuck	sticking
(to) sting	stung	stung	stinging
(to) stink	stank	stunk	stinking
(to) stride	strode	stridden	striding
(to) strike	struck	struck	striking
(to) string	strung	strung	stringing
(to) strive	strove	striven	striving
(to) swear	swore	sworn	swearing
(to) sweep	swept	swept	sweeping
(to) swell	swelled	swelled/swollen	swelling
(to) swim	swam	swum	swimming
(to) swing	swung	swung	swinging
(to) take	took	taken	taking
(to) teach	taught	taught	teaching

(to) tear	tore	torn	tearing
(to) tell	told	told	telling
(to) think	thought	thought	thinking
(to) thrive	thrived/throve	thrived	thriving
(to) throw	threw	thrown	throwing
(to) thrust	thrust	thrust	thrusting
(to) tread	trod	trodden	treading
(to) understand	understood	understood	understanding
(to) uphold	upheld	upheld	upholding
(to) upset	upset	upset	upsetting
(to) wake	woke	woken	waking
(to) wear	wore	worn	wearing
(to) weave	wove	woven	weaving
(to) wed	wedded, wed	wedded, wed	wedding
(to) weep	wept	wept	weeping
(to) wind	wound	wound	winding
(to) win	won	won	winning
(to) withhold	withheld	withheld	withholding
(to) withstand	withstood	withstood	withstanding
(to) wring	wrung	wrung	wringing
(to) write	wrote	written	writing

ACKNOWLEDGEMENTS

Bellafiore, Joseph *Essentials of English.* Third Edition. New York: Amsco, 1983

Burchfield, R. W. ed. *The New Fowler's Modern English Usage.* Third Edition. Oxford: Clarendon Press, 1996

Evler, Mescal ed. *English Workshop: Fourth Course .* Austin: Holt, Rinehart and Winston, 1995

Fowler, H. Ramsey and Aaron, Jane E. *The Little, Brown Handbook.* Seventh Edition. New York: Longman, 1998

Fox, Edward J. Jr. and Moore, Malcom T. *Words, Phrases, and Clauses: Exercises in English Grammar.* Concord: Wayside, 1996

Gorrell, Donna *The Little, Brown Workbook.* Seventh Edition.
New York: Longman, 1998

Hacker, Diana *A Pocket Style Manual.* Second Edition. Boston: Bedford Books, 1997

Hale, Constance *Wired Style: Principles of English Usage in the Digital Age.* San Francisco: Hard Wired, 1996

Harmon, William and Holman, C. Hugh *A Handbook to Literature.* Seventh Edition. Upper Saddle River: Prentice Hall, 1996

Myers, John A. Jr. and Marshall, Carol *The Range of Literature: Poetry.* Boston: Houghton Mifflin, 1969

Strunk, William Jr. and White, E.B. *The Elements of Style.* Third Edition. New York: MacMillan, 1979

Warriner, John E. *English Grammar and Composition: Fourth Course.* Orlando: Harcourt Brace Jovanovich, 1982

We owe special thanks to David Zivan, Peter Hare, Nanette and Michael Giles, Beth Lyon, Linda Lew, Nicky Cohen, Alex Nakahara, Gene Moutous, Alex Pearson, Lee Pearcy, Mike Klaassan, Molly Konopka, Mary Allen, Tim Kent, Mark Luff, Rick Knox, Tom Greenwood, and Alan Hume and the Class of 1944.